Graceful
Goodies

Contents

Introduction

Ever since I was a little girl I have loved baking. As a fisherman's daughter I was brought up on the water so much of my baking on the boat meant my sister and I had to improvise. I remember using a lemonade bottle as a rolling pin to make pastry for apple pies to eat after our fishing expeditions. You always work up an appetite on the water and anything sweet was always gratefully received after a long haul on the boat. Being my father's daughter it was impossible to escape the influence of his sweet tooth.

When I was only about 8 years old, I had set my heart on making a birthday cake for my dad in the shape of his boat. We lived out in the country back then and suffered many long power cuts. One night we suffered a particularly long one. In my determination to make dad's cake I mixed all the ingredients, popped them in baking tins and made my dad drive me to my grandparents' house in the next village along. To my relief they still had electricity so I used their oven to bake the cake and returned home to put it altogether, cut it into the boat shape and then iced and decorated it under the candle light. Where there's a will there's a way!

Since that day my love for baking has continued to grow. I dread to think of the calories consumed over the years and how many cakes I have baked in my time. I take a recipe, I try it, I adapt it to give it the 'Stacey Twist', I try it again , maybe tweak it for a second or even third time and keep going until it gets the seal of approval from my husband in the form of a very satisfying smile of contentment.

After several attempts of nearly killing my husband off with some eccentric adaptations to my recipes, when I'm fairly confident that they are finally safe to share with the public, I will cautiously serve them on board Lady Grace with a warning label:

"Compliments to the Skipper, Complaints to Cakes Anonymous".

While waiting in anticipation to see how many will keel over from my wacky baking we enjoy watching the wading birds amongst the mudflats as the sun drops below the horizon.

This book hasn't got your traditional photos of cake results, instead; I share with you all the amazing views of nature: landscapes, sunrises and sunsets I have been lucky enough to experience on Lady Grace whilst enjoying these sweet seaside sensations. The recipes within are my most favourite and frequently used recipes for you to try for yourselves. Using plain and simple ingredients you'd find in your cupboard, no need to trawl through the supermarkets for expensive or fancy ingredients. So get baking and enjoy!

Luscious Lunchbox Surprises

Belgium Buns

Despite there being a few processes to this particular recipe, it is in fact very simple and exceptionally rewarding. If you make the dough during the evening you can pop these straight in the oven the next morning while you're eating breakfast and they'll be ready to pop in your lunchbox before you leave for work.

For the dough:

400g plain flour

1tsp dried yeast

55ml water

100ml milk

50g butter

1 egg

2 pinches salt

30g caster sugar

½ tsp vanilla extract

1tbsp milk for brushing

For the filling:

400g jar of lemon curd

2 handfuls of mixed dried fruit

For the topping:

6 glace cherries

1 cup of icing sugar

2-3tbsp water

Line two 20cm loose bottomed round tins with greaseproof paper. Generously grease a bowl ready to pop the dough into for the proving process. Have a rolling pin to hand.

1. Put the milk, water and butter into a bowl and pop in the microwave for 30 seconds or until the butter has melted and the milk and water is lukewarm temperature.

2. Put all the dough ingredients into a bowl and using an electric whisk with kneading prongs knead the mixture into a dough for approx. 10 minutes until it forms a ball of dough.

3. Put the dough mix into a well-greased bowl and cover with cling film.

4. Leave the dough to rest at room temperature for an hour and a half. If your house is quite cold, pop it in the airing cupboard. When you return to your dough it should have doubled in size.

5. Lightly flour your worktop and roll out the dough into a rectangular shape so that it is about 5mm thick.

6. If you are making your own lemon curd, please follow the recipe on page 79. Using a metal spoon mix the lemon curd in the jar until

4

it is of a spreadable consistency and spoon the curd generously onto the dough, spreading evenly using the back of the spoon.

7. Sprinkle the dried fruit over the lemon curd.

8. Roll the dough up along its length to create a long sausage shape.

9. Cut into 12 equal slices, placing 6 slices in each lined tin leaving a small gap between each slice giving them room to expand.

10. Brush them with milk and cover with cling film and leave them at room temperature again for about an hour. I normally make these in the evening so at this stage I will leave them in an airtight container overnight in the fridge.

11. Turn on the oven to 200°C and bake for 20 minutes or until they are golden brown. Now because these must be eaten the same day, at this point you could just bake 1 tin of 6 slices and leave the other tin in the fridge for the next day if you only have a small group to share them with or you're not feeling that hungry.

12. Once they have started cooling down mix the icing sugar with water to make a thick but spreadable icing.

13. The slices will probably have moulded together slightly when they expanded so using a knife cut them apart and place them onto a plate.

14. Using a teaspoon, spoon a couple of teaspoons of icing onto each slice and spread using the back of the spoon. Don't worry if the icing sugar runs down the sides of the slices, it makes them look even more scrumptious.

15. Chop the cherries into halves and place one half on each slice and pop in your lunchbox.

Peanut Butter Cupcakes

These are for those with an exceptionally sweet tooth. They are always requested on my tea and cakes sunset boat trips, I cannot turn up without them. Very simple to make, no cooking required and they certainly make your mouth water!

Ingredients

For the base:

200g icing sugar

200g peanut butter

55g butter

55g demerara sugar

For the topping:

300g dark chocolate

Fill a 12 hole cupcake tray with 12 paper cases.

1. Put all the base ingredients into a bowl and mix together into a sandy texture.

2. Using a metal teaspoon spoon the mixture evenly between the 12 paper cases.

3. Using the back of the spoon, compress the mixture to form the base of the cake.

4. Break up the chocolate into a bowl and pop in the microwave on a medium setting for approx. 1 minute until all the chocolate is melted.

5. Pour the melted chocolate over the peanut butter bases and shake the tin to smooth and level out the chocolate topping.

6. Pop in the fridge for 45 minutes until the chocolate has set and then they are ready for eating. They are lovely with a cup of tea. I'd love to know how many you can eat in one sitting, my record is 3 cakes; can you break it?

Egg Custard Tarts

These are one of my Scotty's favourites! You can use half cream and half milk to give that light wobbly centre or you can substitute the milk and use all cream in this recipe for a creamier yet denser texture.

Ingredients

For the pastry:

225g plain flour

110g butter at room temperature

80g caster sugar

2-3tbsp water

For the filling:

150ml double cream

150ml full fat milk

2 eggs plus 1 egg yolk

25g caster sugar

For the topping:

1tsp ground nutmeg

Turn the oven on to 170°C while you make your pastry and filling. Grease a 12 hole cupcake tray.

1. Put all the pastry ingredients into a bowl and using your fingertips rub the butter into the flour and sugar.

2. Once the mixture starts to form fine bread crumbs using your hands start to compress the mixture together adding water as required to form a soft ball of dough. It is very important that your butter is at room temperature otherwise the mixture will not form the right consistency.

3. Roll out the pastry onto a lightly floured surface.

4. Using a 10cm round frilly edged pastry cutter, cut out 12 circles.

5. Line the 12 hole cupcake tray with a circle pastry in each, compressing the pastry against the sides and the bottom of each well.

5. Using a non-stick saucepan, heat the milk and cream until it is warm, remembering to stir it frequently to avoid burning the bottom of the saucepan.

6. Beat in the eggs, egg yolk and sugar into the milk and cream.

7. Pour in the creamy mixture into the pastry cases, filling each case to the brim.

8. Sprinkle generously with nutmeg.

9. Pop in the oven and bake for 15-20 minutes, until the custard has set so when you wobble the tray the custard doesn't wobble.

10. Allow the tarts to cool down before turning out of the tray.

11. Once they have cooled down pop them in an airtight container in the fridge until you are ready to fill your lunchbox.

Streusel Cake

This is a lovely light sponge topped with a crunchy, nutty cinnamon topping. Absolutely divine!

Ingredients

For the sponge:

225g self-raising flour

225g caster sugar

225g butter

4 eggs

1tsp vanilla essence

For the topping:

25g butter

75g demerara sugar

1tsp ground cinnamon

50g mixed nuts

25g self-raising flour

Turn the oven on to 180°C while you make the mixture. Using greaseproof paper; line approx. 30cm x 20cm rectangular oven proof dish (or similar size). Make sure the greaseproof paper overhangs the long edges of the dish.

For the sponge:

1. Cream the butter and sugar together using a wooden spoon.

2. Beat in the eggs.

3. Add the flour and mix until even.

4. Add the vanilla essence and mix until even.

5. Pour mixture into the lined dish.

For the topping:

6. Put the butter, sugar, cinnamon and flour into a bowl and rub together.

7. Finely chop the nuts and mix into the flour and sugar.

8. Sprinkle the nutty mixture on top of the sponge batter mix and pop in the oven.

9. Set the timer to 30 minutes and when it beeps take the cake out of the oven and using a skewer check if it comes out cleanly when inserted into the centre of the mix. If yes, turn the oven off and proceed to step 7, if no; cover with tinfoil and pop back in the oven for a further 10 minutes or until a skewer comes out cleanly.

10. Using the overhanging greaseproof paper from the long edges of the dish; lift out the cake carefully. Cut the cake into even slices and serve hot or cold.

Chocolate Muffins

These are very moist and can last up to a week if stored in an airtight container, mind you; they'll never last a week in my house!

Ingredients

115g plain flour

175g caster sugar

40g cocoa powder

1½ tsp baking powder

1 egg

125ml milk

60ml vegetable oil

1 tsp vanilla extract

125ml boiling water

Turn the oven on to 180°C while you make your mixture. Fill a 12 hole cupcake tray with 12 paper cases.

1. Put all the ingredients EXCEPT the boiling water in a bowl and using an electric whisk whiz it all together on a high speed creating air bubbles in the mixture.

2. Turn the electric whisk down to a very slow speed and gradually add the boiling water until it's all evenly mixed together. The mixture will now be a very runny batter.

3. Pour the mixture into the 12 paper cases dividing it evenly between them.

4. Pop the tray in the oven and bake for 20 minutes.

5. Remove from the oven and turn out onto a wire rack to cool.

14

Battenberg

Just for fun I like to jazz this recipe up a little and change the chequered colours to purple or blue every once in a while.

Ingredients

100g butter

100g caster sugar

2 eggs

50g ground rice

100g self-raising flour

½ tsp baking powder

1tsp almond essence

Red food colouring

5-6tbsp strawberry jam

225g marzipan

Turn the oven on to 160°C while you make your mixture. Line 2 loaf tins with greaseproof paper.

1. Cream the butter and sugar together using a wooden spoon.

2. Beat in the eggs.

3. Add the flour, baking powder and ground rice, mix together to a batter.

4. Add a couple of drops of almond essence and mix again.

5. Divide the mixture up into equal halves.

6. Add a couple of drops of red food colouring to one half and mix until the colour is flowing evenly through the mix, or if you fancy a different colour instead of red – go for it!

7. Pour the red mix into one of the lined loaf tins and the plain mix into the other lined tin.

8. Pop into the oven for approx. 20 minutes or until a skewer comes out cleanly then remove from the oven.

9. Wait for the cakes to cool down before you turn them out.

10. Once you have turned the cakes out, cut them both equally down the middle, long ways, so you have 4 long thin cake slices.

11. Using a knife beat the jam in the jar to make it runny and spreadable and spread it generously over the 4 slices of cake, on top and on the edges and place the cakes together in a chequered pattern.

12. Roll the marzipan into an oblong big and wide enough to wrap the cake in.

13. Using a metal spoon, add some jam onto the marzipan and spread evenly with the back of the spoon.

14. Gently lift the chequered cake onto the marzipan and roll it up, make sure the joining edge is on the bottom of the cake unseen.

15. Sprinkle with caster sugar and cut into slices for your lunchbox.

Swiss Roll

If I fancy something sweet and I've run out of butter this is the perfect answer to my cravings. Very simple but exceptionally satisfying. You can substitute the jam for lemon curd if you fancy giving it a try.

Ingredients

3 eggs

75g caster sugar

75g self-raising flour

150-200g strawberry jam

Turn the oven on to 200°C while you make your mixture. Using greaseproof paper; line a swiss roll tray if you have one, if not; approx. 30cm x 20cm rectangular oven proof dish (or similar size). Make sure the greaseproof paper overhangs the long edges of the dish.

1. Put the eggs in a bowl and whisk for 2 minutes.

2. Add the sugar and continue to whisk on a high speed for a further 10 minutes or until the mixture is very light in colour, doubled in volume and thick in texture to the consistency of a softly whipped cream.

3. Using a metal spoon, very gently fold in the flour so that you don't beat the air out of the mixture.

4. Pour into the prepared tin and pop in the over for approx. 12 minutes or until well risen and firm to touch.

5. Now you need to act quick, make sure your filling of jam is ready to hand when the swiss roll comes out of the oven.

6. Turn out the swiss roll onto a lightly sugared surface and peel off the greaseproof paper.

7. Using a knife mix the jam in the jar until it is of a spreadable consistency and spread evenly over the rectangular sponge. You want to see the filling oozing out the end so make sure you're generous with your filling.

8. Taking the short edge, roll up tightly and place on a plate with the joining edge hiding underneath.

9. Sprinkle with caster sugar and slice to serve.

If you fancy a jam and cream filling:

At the end of step 6; use a sheet of greaseproof paper to roll the swiss roll with and leave the filling out so it's just paper inside, wait for it to cool down completely then unroll and fill with jam and cream before re-rolling up.

Flapjacks

The good old flapjack, baking doesn't get simpler than this.

Ingredients

340g butter

340g demerara sugar

450g porridge oats

1-2 handfuls of raisins (optional)

Turn the oven on to 180°C while you make your mixture. Grease a 20cm loose bottom round tin.

1. Using a non-stick saucepan; put the butter and sugar over a low heat and melt slowly until the sugar dissolves, stirring with a wooden spoon frequently to ensure the sugar doesn't burn on the bottom of the pan.

2. Take the saucepan off the heat and add the oats to the mixture. Stir well until it is evenly mixed. If you are adding raisins to your flapjacks, now's the time.

3. Pour into the tin and press down lightly to compact the mixture.

4. Pop in the oven for 20 minutes.

5. Leave it to cool down before cutting into triangle slices.

Butterfly Cakes

I remember making these all the time as a little girl for dad when he'd come in from fishing. The 'Stacey Twist' is the secret jam inside hidden under the buttercream.

Ingredients

170g self-raising flour

170g caster sugar

170g butter

3 eggs

1tsp vanilla essence

12 tsp strawberry jam

Vanilla butter icing from page 79

Multi-coloured candy strands (optional decoration)

Turn the oven on to 180°C while you make your sponge mix. Line a 12 hole cupcake tray with paper cases.

1. Cream the butter and sugar together using a wooden spoon.

2. Beat in the eggs.

3. Add the flour and mix until even.

4. Add the vanilla essence and mix again.

5. Spoon the mixture into the paper cake cases.

6. Pop in the oven for 15-20 minutes or until a skewer comes out cleanly when inserted into the centre of the cake.

7. Turn out onto a wire rack and start cutting the round slices out of the top of the cakes which will allow them to cool down quicker. Make sure you cut the slices deep so that we can fit plenty of filling inside.

8. Cut each round slice into halves for the butterfly wings.

9. Using a teaspoon, place 1 teaspoon of jam into each cake.

10. Make your vanilla butter icing using the recipe on page 79.

11. Using a clean teaspoon, place a heaped teaspoon of butter icing mixture over the top covering up the jam.

12. Place the halved slices onto the icing at an angle to form wings.

13. Sprinkle multi-coloured candy strands over the butter icing to decorate.

Rock Cakes

Who doesn't love to open their lunchbox and be greeted by a rock cake?

Ingredients

225g self-raising flour

100g butter

75g caster sugar

100g mixed dried fruit

1 egg

50g glace cherries

Turn the oven on to 200°C while you make the mixture. Grease a baking tray.

1. Rub the butter and flour together to make fine breadcrumbs.

2. Add the sugar and mixed fruit.

3. Using a sharp knife, cut the cherries into halves and add into the flour mix.

4. Beat the egg in a separate bowl.

5. Add the egg to the flour and fruit mix until it forms a doughy ball.

6. Using a metal spoon, place 8 spoonful's of mixture, in rocky round shapes, equally spaced apart onto the lined baking tray.

7. Pop the tray in the oven for 20 minutes.

8. Sprinkle with caster sugar and pack in your lunchbox.

Cinnamon Swirls

I am told by a very good friend of mine that; if you like these you will DEFINITELY like my Nutella and hazelnut swirls so you MUST try them. Substitute the below filling for a jar of Nutella and a handful of chopped hazelnuts, no topping required.

For the dough:

400g plain flour

1tsp dried yeast

55ml water

100ml milk

50g butter

1 egg

2 pinches salt

30g caster sugar

½ tsp vanilla extract

1tbsp milk for brushing

For the filling:

60g caster sugar

5 tsp ground cinnamon

2tbsp melted butter

For the topping:

100g icing sugar

100g soft cheese

Line two 20cm loose bottomed round tins with greaseproof paper. Generously grease a bowl ready to pop the dough into for the proving process. Have a rolling pin to hand.

1. Put the milk, water and butter into a bowl and pop in the microwave for 30 seconds or until the butter has melted and the milk and water is lukewarm temperature.

2. Put all the dough ingredients into a bowl and using an electric whisk with kneading prongs knead the mixture into a dough and continuing kneading for approx. 10 minutes.

3. Put the dough mix into a well-greased bowl and cover with cling film.

4. Leave the dough to rest at room temperature for an hour and a half. If your house is quite cold, pop it in the airing cupboard. When you return to your dough it should have doubled in size.

5. Lightly flour your worktop and roll out the dough into a rectangular shape so that it is about 5mm thick.

6. Brush the dough with melted butter.

7. Mix the cinnamon and sugar in a bowl until evenly mixed then sprinkle the sugar and spice over the dough.

8. Roll the dough up along its length to create a long sausage shape.

9. Cut into 12 equal slices, placing 6 slices in each lined tin leaving a small gap between each slice giving them room to expand.

10. Brush them with milk and cover with cling film and leave them at room temperature again for about an hour. I normally make these in the evening so at this stage I will leave them overnight in the fridge.

11. Turn on the oven to 200°C and bake for 20 minutes or until they are golden brown. Now because these must be eaten the same day, at this point you could just bake 1 tin of 6 slices and leave the other tin in the fridge for the next day if you only have a small group to share them with or you're not feeling that hungry.

12. Once they have started cooling down mix the icing sugar with the soft cheese.

13. The slices will probably have moulded together slightly when they expanded so using a knife cut them apart and place them onto a plate.

14. Using a teaspoon, spoon a couple of teaspoons of icing onto each slice and spread using the back of the spoon.

Delicious Dinner Desserts

Mint Chocolate Marble Cake

Ingredients

For the chocolate part:

115g plain flour

175g caster sugar

40g cocoa powder

1½ tsp baking powder

1 egg

125ml milk

60ml vegetable oil

1 tsp vanilla extract

125ml boiling water

For the mint part:

115g self-raising flour

115g caster sugar

115g butter

2 eggs

1tsp peppermint extract

You cannot make this without colouring the mint part green otherwise it just won't taste the same.

2-3 drops of green food colouring

To decorate:

1-2 squares of dark chocolate (leaving the rest for you to munch on while you cook)

2 drops of peppermint extract

1-2 drops of green food colouring

1 cup of icing sugar

2-3tbsp water

Chocolate butter icing from page 81

Turn the oven on to 180°C while you make your mixture. Using Greaseproof paper; line two 20cm loose bottomed round tins.

For the chocolate part:

1. Put all the ingredients EXCEPT the boiling water in a bowl and using an electric whisk whiz it all together on a high speed creating air bubbles in the mixture.

2. Turn the electric whisk down to a very slow speed and gradually add the boiling water until it's all evenly mixed together. The mixture will now be very runny.

For the mint part:

3. In a separate bowl; cream the butter and sugar together using a wooden spoon.

4. Beat in the eggs.

5. Add the flour and mix until even.

6. Add the peppermint extract and a couple of drops of green food colouring and mix again.

7. Using a metal spoon, place spoonful's of the mint mixture at the clock positions, 12, 3, 6 and 9 into the lined tins and a spoonful in the centres too.

8. Using the chocolate mixture fill the rest of the gaps in the tins between the green mix spoonful's.

9. Pop the tins in the oven and bake for 25-30 minutes or until a skewer comes out cleanly when inserted into the centre of the cake.

10. Remove from the oven and turn out onto a wire rack to cool. This is a really light fluffy moist cake so unfortunately you might have the odd bit of sponge fall off round the edges or stick to the greaseproof paper when you peel it off so be sure to gobble up any crumbs. Be patient and do not ice the cake too early, make sure it has cooled down before you attempt icing it.

11. HALF the chocolate butter icing recipe from page 81 to make the filling for the cake

12. Mix the icing sugar with water, add the drops of peppermint and green food colour to make a thick but spreadable icing.

13. Use the chocolate butter icing to fill and sandwich the 2 cakes together.

14. Using the green peppermint icing, spread over the top of the cake and use the back of a knife to spread and smooth the icing to make it look neat.

15. Grate the squares of plain chocolate over the top to decorate.

Bakewell

A chunky slice of Bakewell served with a generous helping of thick custard is a real homely comfort food.

Ingredients

For the pastry:

225g plain flour

110g butter at room temperature

80g caster sugar

2-3tbsp water

For the filling:

115g self-raising flour

115g caster sugar

115g butter

2 eggs

2tsp almond extract

100g ground almonds

250g raspberry jam

For the topping:

100g flaked almonds

Turn the oven on to 180°C while you make your pastry and filling. Grease a 22cm round ovenproof dish.

For the pastry:

1. Put all the pastry ingredients into a bowl and using your fingertips rub the butter into the flour and sugar.

2. Once the mixture starts to form fine bread crumbs using your hands start to compress the mixture together adding water as required to form a ball of dough. It is very important that your butter is at room temperature otherwise the mixture will form the right consistency.

3. Roll out the pastry onto a lightly floured surface.

4. Using your fingertips to lift the edge of the pastry and slide the rolling pin underneath, lift the pastry over the greased round tin and compress round the edges of the tin.

5. Cut off any excess pastry round the top.

For the filling:

6. Using a metal spoon, spoon in the jam and spread evenly over the pastry base.

7. Cream the butter and sugar together using a wooden spoon.

8. Beat in the eggs.

9. Add the flour and mix until even.

10. Add the ground almonds and almond extract and mix until even.

11. Pour the mixture over the top of the jam and spread evenly making sure all the jam is covered.

12. Sprinkle the flaked almonds on top neatly for decoration.

13. Pop in the oven and bake for 50 minutes until it is firm to touch and a skewer comes out clean when inserted into the centre of the cake.

14. Remove from the oven and wait for it to cool down.

If you serve this before it has had time to cool down a bit then the jam is still very runny so just be prepared to get messy and if you do make sure you lick those fingers!

Bread Pudding

This is one of my husband's favourites to get from the bakery so it was a recipe that required perfecting at my earliest ability. It works best with stale bread and crusts which is really handy as I hate waste in the kitchen so I freeze down all my crusts until I have saved a whole bag full and then I get baking. It makes the whole house smell of Christmas with the spices that greet you as you enter.

800g stale bread (2 loaves)

200g caster sugar

350g butter

10tbsp ground mixed spice

250ml lemon juice

4 eggs

700g dried mixed fruit

Turn the oven on to 180°C while you make the mixture. Using greaseproof paper; line approx. 35cmx24cm rectangular oven proof dish (or similar size). Make sure the greaseproof paper overhangs the long edges of the dish.

1. Soak the bread in a bowl of lukewarm water until soggy.

2. Using your hands; compress the bread between your palms to squeeze out excess water.

3. Using your fingertips; break up the bread into an empty bowl.

4. Again, using your fingertips; break up the butter into small pieces and add to the bread bowl.

5. Add the caster sugar, dried mixed fruit and spice.

6. Beat the eggs in a bowl and then add to the bread mix along with the lemon juice.

7. Using your hands or a big spoon, mix up all the ingredients until they are evenly mixed.

8. Pour the mixture into the lined dish and pop in the oven for 40 minutes or until it is firm to touch.

9. Wait until the pudding has cooled down before turning out. Using the overhanging greaseproof paper from the long edges of the dish; lift out the cake carefully.

10. Cut the pudding into even slices and sprinkle with caster sugar. Be sure to serve with clotted cream for the wow factor.

34

Chocolate Fudge Cake

This is a very rewardingly moist chocolatey cake, not for the faint hearted. You'll feel like you've cheated – it's so easy to make.

Ingredients

225g plain flour

350g caster sugar

85g cocoa powder

1½ tsp baking powder

1½ tsp bicarbonate of soda

2 eggs

250ml milk

125ml vegetable oil

2 tsp vanilla extract

250ml boiling water

Turn the oven on to 180°C while you make your mixture. Using Greaseproof paper; line two 20cm loose bottomed round tins.

1. Put all the ingredients EXCEPT the boiling water in a bowl and using an electric whisk whiz it all together on a high speed creating air bubbles in the mixture.

2. Turn the electric whisk down to a very slow speed and gradually add the boiling water until it's all evenly mixed together. The mixture will now be very runny.

3. Pour the mixture into the 2 tins dividing it evenly between them.

4. Pop the tins in the oven and bake for 20-25 minutes or until a skewer comes out cleanly when inserted into the centre of the cake.

5. Remove from the oven and turn out onto a wire rack to cool. This is a really light fluffy moist cake so unfortunately you might have the odd bit of sponge fall off round the edges or stick to the greaseproof paper when you peel it off so be sure to gobble up any crumbs. Be patient and do not ice the cake too early, make sure it has cooled down before you attempt icing it.

6. Use chocolate butter icing recipe from page 81 to make the filling and topping.

7. Use half the icing mix to fill and sandwich the 2 cakes together.

8. Using the remaining icing, spread over the top of the cake and use the back of a knife to spread and smooth the icing to make it look neat.

9. You can now serve the cake as it is or you can get fancy and chop strawberries in half (leaving the leaves in for decorative purposes) and place them on the top to make it look pretty. Chocolate and strawberries makes for an amazing combination, it's an explosion of flavours in your mouth.

Marmalade Pudding

This pudding has a deliciously light texture of a steamed pudding with a zesty flavour. It's lovely served straight from the oven with custard or cream or equally as nice in your lunchbox cold the next day.

500g butter

150g caster sugar

150g light brown muscovado sugar

8 eggs

450g self-raising flour

900g marmalade (1.5 jars for inside the cake and half a jar for on top of the cake)

Turn the oven on to 180°C while you make the mixture. Using greaseproof paper; line approx. 35cmx24cm rectangular oven proof dish (or similar size). Make sure the greaseproof paper overhangs the long edges of the dish.

1. Cream the butter and sugars together using a wooden spoon.

2. Beat in the eggs.

3. Add the flour and mix until even.

4. Add one whole jar of marmalade and half of the other jar and mix until even.

5. Pour mixture into the lined dish and pop in the oven.

6. Set the timer to 45 minutes and when it beeps take the cake out of the oven and using a skewer check if it comes out cleanly when inserted into the centre of the mix. If yes, turn the oven off and proceed to step 7, if no; cover with tinfoil and pop back in the oven for a further 15 minutes or until a skewer comes out cleanly.

7. While the cake is still piping hot, using a metal spoon beat the remaining marmalade in the jar to make it runny and spreadable. Spoon the marmalade over the cake and using the back of the spoon spread the marmalade generously across the top of the cake until it is evenly covered.

8. Using the overhanging greaseproof paper from the long edges of the dish; lift out the cake carefully. Cut the cake into even slices and serve hot or cold.

Rhubarb Crumble Cake

Served hot or cold this has a lovely contrast of sweet crumble and cake mixed with the sharpness of the rhubarb. If you're serving it hot you must add a dollop of dairy ice cream!

For the cake:

100g butter

100g caster sugar

150g self-raising flour

40ml milk

2 eggs

For the filling:

1 rhubarb stem

For the crumble:

120g butter

120g demerara sugar

150g plain flour

Turn the oven on to 180°C while you make your mixture. Grease a deep 18cm loose bottomed round tin.

For the cake:

1. Cream the butter and sugar together using a wooden spoon.

2. Beat in the eggs.

3. Add the flour and mix until even.

4. Add the milk and mix again.

5. Pour mixture into the tin.

For the filling:

6. Chop the rhubarb stem into even slices and push down into the cake mix evenly spaced apart.

For the crumble:

7. Rub the flour and butter together to a breadcrumb texture.

8. Add the sugar and mix together.

9. Sprinkle crumble mix over the top of the cake and pop in the oven.

6. After 30 minutes take the cake out and pop a tinfoil cover over the top for the remaining half hour to ensure the crumble doesn't go too brown on top.

7. Turn the oven off and leave the cake in the oven for a further 20 minutes before taking out to serve.

Fruit Scones

You must serve these with strawberry jam and clotted cream – it's the rules!

Ingredients

225g self-raising flour

50g butter

150ml milk

50g sultanas

25g caster sugar

Turn the oven on to 230°C while you make your mixture. Grease a baking tray.

1. Using your fingertips; rub the butter and flour together until it resembles fine breadcrumbs.

2. Add the sugar and sultanas and mix evenly.

3. Add the milk and use a metal spoon to stir it into a soft but not sticky dough.

4. Roll out the dough onto a lightly floured surface to approx. 1cm thick.

5. Using a 6.5cm round frilly edged pastry cutter, cut into rounds and pop on to the greased baking tray evenly spaced apart.

6. Brush the tops with milk before popping in the oven and baking for approx. 10 minutes until they are well risen and golden brown.

7. Turn out onto a wire rack to cool down and serve.

Rice Pudding

An under-rated dessert, a great comfort food, must be served with a big spoonful of raspberry jam.

Ingredients

125g pudding rice

800ml milk preferably full fat

2tbsp caster sugar

1tsp vanilla essence

1 handful of raisins (optional)

1. Put the rice, milk and vanilla essence into a big non-stick saucepan and bring to the boil on a high heat and ensure you frequently stir it.

2. Turn the hob ring down to a low to medium setting and simmer for 30-40 minutes until the rice has expanded and the milk has reduced.

3. Add the sugar and stir in until the sugar has dissolved.

4. Remove the pan from the heat.

5. If you wish to add raisins to your rice pudding, add these now and stir the pudding again.

6. If you are serving this hot; divide into dishes, add a generous dollop of raspberry jam and serve. If you are serving this cold you may want to add extra milk before serving to reduce the thickness to your preference.

Ice Cream

This is seriously creamy and a perfect accompaniment to most desserts in this book! You've got to try it to believe it. You can experiment with flavours of your choice. Perhaps add a dash of rum and a handful of raisins or maybe you'd prefer a few drops of peppermint essence and a handful of chocolate chips.

Ingredients

568ml double cream

4tbsp milk

90g icing sugar

2tsp vanilla essence

1. Pour the cream and milk into a bowl and whisk at a high speed until it forms soft peaks.

2. Stir in the icing sugar and vanilla essence.

3. Pop into an airtight container suitable for the freezer and leave in the freezer for at least 3 hours before attempting to eat it.

44

Raspberry Jam and Coconut Sponge

This recipe reminds me of my dad, he loves anything coconutty. When we were little we'd go in the old fashioned sweet shops and we always come out with coconut mushrooms just for dad.

Ingredients

For the sponge:

225g self-raising flour

225g caster sugar

225g butter

4 eggs

1tsp vanilla essence

120g desiccated coconut

For the topping:

450g raspberry jam

80g desiccated coconut

Turn the oven on to 180°C while you make the mixture. Using greaseproof paper; line approx. 30cm x 20cm rectangular oven proof dish (or similar size). Make sure the greaseproof paper overhangs the long edges of the dish.

1. Cream the butter and sugar together using a wooden spoon.

2. Beat in the eggs.

3. Add the flour and mix until even.

4. Add 120g of the desiccated coconut and vanilla essence and mix until even.

5. Pour mixture into the lined dish and pop in the oven.

6. Set the timer to 30 minutes and when it beeps take the cake out of the oven and using a skewer check if it comes out cleanly when inserted into the centre of the mix. If yes, turn the oven off and proceed to step 7, if no; cover with tinfoil and pop back in the oven for a further 10 minutes or until a skewer comes out cleanly.

7. While the cake is still piping hot, using a metal spoon beat the raspberry jam in the jar to make it runny and spreadable. Spoon the jam over the cake and using the back of the spoon spread the jam generously across the top of the cake until it is evenly covered.

8. Using the remaining 80g of desiccated coconut; sprinkle it evenly over the top of the jam.

9. Using the overhanging greaseproof paper from the long edges of the dish; lift out the cake carefully. Cut the cake into even slices and serve hot or cold.

46

Banoffee Pie

This is so easy to make but very impressive when served up and tasted! As I type this recipe I am itching to get in the kitchen and make this for Scott's tea tonight.

Ingredients

For the base:

300g hobnob biscuits (1 pack) or digestives if you prefer

100g butter

For the filling:

397g can of Carnation caramel

3-4 bananas

For the topping:

284ml double cream

1 square of milk or dark chocolate

20cm loose bottomed round tin

1. Crush the biscuits into crumbs.

2. Put the butter in a bowl in the microwave onto a medium to high heat setting for 1 minute.

3. Take out the microwave and stir, if not completely melted, put back in the microwave for 15 seconds and repeat until fully melted.

4. Mix together the biscuit crumbs and the melted butter.

5. Pour into the tin and using the back of a metal spoon press lightly to evenly spread and compress the mixture to form the base.

6. Spread the caramel over the base evenly.

7. Slice the bananas and add on top of the caramel.

8. Whip the cream until it forms soft peaks.

9. Spread the cream over the bananas.

10. Grate chocolate over the top and store in the fridge until ready to serve.

Black Cherry Cheesecake

This is always a winner when you are throwing a dinner party.

Ingredients

For the base:

100g butter

300g hobnob biscuits (1 pack) or digestives if you prefer

For the filling:

200g soft cheese

120g caster sugar

284ml double cream

For the topping:

410g black cherry fruit filling (1 tin)

18cm loose bottomed round tin

1. Crush the biscuits into crumbs.

2. Put the butter in a bowl in the microwave onto a medium to high heat setting for 1 minute.

3. Take out the microwave and stir, if not completely melted, put back in the microwave for 15 seconds and repeat until fully melted.

4. Mix together the biscuit crumbs and the melted butter.

5. Pour into the tin and using the back of a metal spoon press lightly to evenly spread and compress the mixture to form the base.

6. Put the cream, cheese and sugar into a bowl and whisk on a fast speed until soft peaks form.

7. Spread the cream over the base evenly.

8. Spoon the black cherry filling over the top and pop in the fridge for an hour or until you're ready to serve.

Lemon Cheesecake

This is a really citrussy, light and creamy dessert. If you think you're full from dinner, you'll still fit a slice of this in too!

Ingredients

For the base:

100g butter

300g hobnob biscuits (1 pack) or digestives if you prefer

For the filling:

200g soft cheese

397g can of condensed milk

6tbsp lemon juice

For the topping:

6tbsp lemon curd

1tspb water

18cm loose bottomed round tin

1. Crush the biscuits into crumbs.

2. Put the butter in a bowl in the microwave onto a medium to high heat setting for 1 minute.

3. Take out the microwave and stir, if not completely melted, put back in the microwave for 15 seconds and repeat until fully melted.

4. Mix together the biscuit crumbs and the melted butter.

5. Pour into the tin and using the back of a metal spoon press lightly to evenly spread and compress the mixture to form the base.

6. Put the condensed milk and cheese into a bowl and whisk on a fast speed until evenly mixed.

7. Add the lemon juice and whisk again on a slightly lower speed and watch as the mixture starts to thicken.

8. Once forming soft peaks, stop whisking and spread the cream over the base evenly.

9. Chill in the fridge for a couple of hours.

10. Add the lemon curd and water into a small cup or beaker, ping in the microwave for 10-15 seconds to warm slightly.

11. Take the lemon curd out of the microwave and mix the water and curd together before drizzling it over the cheesecake and serving.

Upside Down Cake

As a nice alternative you can substitute the golden syrup and pineapple rings for halved and peeled pears with raspberry jam

Ingredients

115g self-raising flour

115g caster sugar

115g butter

2 eggs

1tsp vanilla essence

3tbsp golden syrup

227g tin of pineapple rings

5 glace cherries

Turn the oven on to 180°C while you make your sponge mix. Line a 20cm round loose bottomed tin with greaseproof paper.

1. Cream the butter and sugar together using a wooden spoon.

2. Beat in the eggs.

3. Add the flour and mix until even.

4. Add the vanilla essence, mix again then set aside.

5. Place 4 pineapple rings evenly apart at the base of the lined tin.

6. Cut the glace cherries into halves and place a cherry half in the centre of each pineapple ring and then one in the centre of the cake and the others around the edge of the cake evenly distributed. Making sure to place the cherries round side down, so cut side facing up.

7. Spoon the golden syrup over the top of the pineapples.

8. Pour the cake mixture evenly over the pineapples.

9. Pop in the oven for 20 minutes or until a skewer comes out cleanly when inserted into the centre of the cake.

10. Leave the cake to cool for 10 minutes or so before inverting it onto a plate.

11. Peel the greaseproof paper off gently.

12. Serve with custard or cream.

Coffee and Walnut Slice

Ingredients

225g self-raising flour

225g caster sugar

225g butter

4 eggs

4tsp coffee granules

1tbsp hot water

50g walnuts

Turn the oven on to 180°C while you make the mixture. Using greaseproof paper; line approx. 30cm x 20cm rectangular oven proof dish (or similar size). Make sure the greaseproof paper overhangs the long edges of the dish.

1. Cream the butter and sugar together using a wooden spoon.

2. Beat in the eggs.

3. Add the flour.

4. Mix the hot water and coffee granules together and pour into the batter and mix until even.

5. Pour mixture into the lined dish and pop in the oven.

6. Pop in the oven for 30 minutes or until a skewer comes out clean when inserted into the centre of the cake.

7. Let the cake cool down completely.

8. Using the overhanging greaseproof paper from the long edges of the dish; lift out the cake carefully.

9. Use the vanilla butter icing recipe from page 79 to make the topping and use the back of a knife to spread and smooth the icing to make it look neat.

10. Chop the walnuts up and sprinkle over the butter icing before it sets. I use scissors to chop the walnuts as it's not so messy and the nuts don't go flying across the worktop like they do when you use a knife and chopping board.

11. Slice the cake and serve

Chocolate Brownies

An absolute all-time favourite, rich, gooey and very chocolatey.
You can add walnuts to this recipe if you wish, I don't but that's just because I'm nutty enough already!

Ingredients

300g white chocolate

300g dark chocolate

225g butter

3 eggs

225g light muscovado sugar

150g self-raising flour

175g walnuts (optional)

Icing sugar to decorate

Turn the oven on to 180°C while you make your mixture. Line approx. 30x20cm rectangular oven proof dish (or similar size). Make sure the greaseproof paper overhangs the long edges of the dish.

1. Using a non-stick saucepan; put the butter and dark chocolate over a low heat and melt slowly, stirring occasionally.

2. Whilst waiting for the butter and chocolate to melt, roughly chop the white chocolate and set aside.

3. Whisk the eggs and the sugar together on a high speed.

4. Add the melted chocolate and butter mix to the eggs and sugar and beat in.

5. Now add the flour and mix together.

6. Pour the batter mix into the dish, sprinkle the white chocolate over the top and pop in the over for approx. 35 minutes or until the centre feels just firm on the crust.

7. Remove from the oven and let it cool down completely.

8. Once it has cooled down, use the overhanging greaseproof paper on the long edges to lift the cake out of the dish and cut into squares and sprinkle with icing sugar to decorate like snow falling on wood in the forests.

Banana and Sultana Cake

This is perfect if you've got a couple of over ripe bananas left over and don't know what to do with them. You can serve this on its own or with a generous dollop of whipped cream.

225g butter

225g caster sugar

4 eggs

225g self-raising flour

2 -3 bananas

2 handfuls of sultanas

Turn the oven on to 180°C while you make your mixture. Grease a deep 18cm loose bottomed round tin.

1. Cream the butter and sugar together using a wooden spoon.

2. Beat in the eggs.

3. Add the flour and mix until even.

4. Add the bananas and sultanas and mix until even.

5. Pour mixture into the tin and pop in the oven.

6. After 30 minutes take the cake out and pop a tinfoil cover over the top for the remaining 15 minutes to ensure the cake doesn't go too brown on top.

7. Take out the oven and using a skewer check if it comes out cleanly when inserted into the centre of the mix. If yes, turn out onto a wire rack to cool down, if no; pop back in the oven for a further 15 minutes or until a skewer comes out cleanly.

Victoria Sponge

Nothing beats plain and simple, this is an absolute all-time favourite. You might like to substitute the jam for real chopped strawberries when they are in season as a refreshing filling.

Ingredients

225g self-raising flour

225g caster sugar

225g butter

4 eggs

1tsp vanilla essence

200g raspberry or strawberry jam

300ml double cream

Icing sugar to decorate

Turn the oven on to 180°C while you make your sponge mix. Grease two 20cm round loose bottomed tins.

1. Cream the butter and sugar together using a wooden spoon.

2. Beat in the eggs.

3. Add the flour and mix until even.

4. Add the vanilla essence and mix again.

5. Pour the mixture evenly between the two tins.

6. Pop in the oven for 20 minutes or until a skewer comes out cleanly when inserted into the centre of the cake.

7. Turn out the cakes onto a wire rack and allow to cool.

8. Whilst your cakes are cooling down, start whipping your cream until it forms soft peaks and place the cream in the fridge until the cake has cooled down.

9. Once the cake is cool, smother the bottom layer with jam and cream and sandwich together.

10. Lightly dust the top of the cake with icing sugar.

62

Lemon Drizzle Slices

Ingredients

For the cake:

225g self-raising flour

225g caster sugar

225g butter

4 eggs

3tbsp lemon juice

For the topping:

1 cup of icing sugar

1tsp lemon juice

2-3tsp water

Turn the oven on to 180°C while you make the mixture. Using greaseproof paper; line approx. 30cm x 20cm rectangular oven proof dish (or similar size). Make sure the greaseproof paper overhangs the long edges of the dish.

1. Cream the butter and sugar together using a wooden spoon.

2. Beat in the eggs.

3. Add the flour.

4. Mix in the lemon juice until even.

5. Pour mixture into the lined dish and pop in the oven for 20 minutes

6. After 20 minutes, remove the cake from the oven quickly and drizzle lemon juice over the sponge generously before popping back in the oven for a further 10 minutes, or until a skewer comes out clean when inserted into the centre of the cake.

7. Let the cake cool down completely.

8. Using the overhanging greaseproof paper from the long edges of the dish; lift out the cake carefully.

9. Mix the icing sugar with the lemon juice and water to make a thick but spreadable icing and use the back of a knife to spread and smooth the icing over the top of the cake to make it look neat.

 10. If you have orange and yellow candy sprinkles you can sprinkle these on top of the icing. or if you have a thin piping nozzle you can mix up some yellow icing and drizzle pinstripe lines of yellow icing over the white icing.

11.Slice the cake and serve.

Stollen

Normally Stollen is quite heavy but I've tweaked my recipe to give a much lighter spongier dough which I prefer.

Ingredients

400g plain flour

1tsp dried yeast

55ml water

100ml milk

50g butter

1 egg

2 pinches salt

30g caster sugar

½ tsp vanilla extract

1tsp ground mace

1tsp mixed spice

175g dried mixed fruit

110g marzipan

For the topping:

1tbsp butter

Icing sugar to decorate

Grease a baking tray with overgenerous amounts of oil.

1. Put the milk, water and butter into a bowl and pop in the microwave for 30 seconds or until the butter has melted and the milk and water is lukewarm temperature.

2. Put all the ingredients into a bowl and using an electric whisk with kneading prongs knead the mixture into a dough and continuing kneading for approx. 10 minutes until the dough forms a ball.

3. On a lightly floured surface, push down on the dough with your palms to flatten the dough into a rectangular shape. Using your hands roll the marzipan into a long thin sausage the same length as the dough and place the marzipan sausage down the middle of the flattened dough. Fold the dough over to encase the marzipan within the dough and place on a baking tray.

4. Using a clean tea towel cover the baking tray and leave in a warm room, I leave mine in the airing cupboard.

5. Leave the dough to rise for 1 hour 30 minutes, I leave mine in the airing cupboard overnight and it rises beautifully to bake the nest morning.

6. Pop in the oven for 45 minutes at 180°C.

7. Put the butter into a bowl and pop in the microwave on a medium to high setting for 20 seconds. If not completely melted, put back in the microwave for 15 seconds and repeat until fully melted

8. Brush with melted butter, dust with icing sugar, slice and serve.

Christmas Pudding/Christmas Cake

This recipe with a bit of marzipan and icing sugar can turn your Christmas pudding into a cake, it's lovely and moist. You can make this up to a year in advance provided you store it in a cool dark place. It does in fact make 2 puddings/cakes so you can make one of each if you like.

Ingredients

750g mixed dried fruit – this can be a mixture of sultanas, raisins, cherries, cranberries, peel

110g dates, stoned and chopped

280g soft brown sugar

110g ground almonds

300ml brandy

3 eggs

85ml stout

110ml self-raising flour

200g shredded suet

140g breadcrumbs

2tsp mixed spice

2tsp ground nutmeg

2tsp ground cinnamon

150ml brandy to light the pudding

You will also need the following if you intend on making the Christmas Cake:

500g marzipan per cake

500g fondant icing per cake

350g jar of apricot jam

Line two pudding bowls with greaseproof paper

1. In a large bowl, put all the dried fruit, dates, sugar and almonds.

2. Pour over the brandy and using a metal spoon mix it all up before covering it over with cling film.

3. Leave it to soak in the fridge overnight, you can leave it longer if you are busy. With my chaotic boat trips I often find I have ended up leaving the fruit soaking for a couple of days, it just gives an even moister result.

4. After the fruit has been left to soak overnight, fill the slow cooker half full with water and turn on high while you make the pudding.

5. Remove the fruit from the fridge.

6. Beat the eggs with the stout then pour over the fruit and mix it altogether with a metal spoon.

7. In a separate bowl, combine the flour, suet, breadcrumbs and spices and mix well.

8. Add the fruit mixture to the flour mix and combine until evenly mixed.

9. Pour the mixture evenly between the 2 bowls and compress down with the back of a metal spoon to fill any empty gaps lower down in the bowl.

10. Cover the top of the bowls with tinfoil then with a separate sheet of tinfoil wrap the whole bowl in tinfoil to help seal it.

11. Place both bowls in the slow cooker, ensuring the water in the slow cooker only comes half way up the side of the bowls, and allow the puddings to steam for 9 hours on high. If the water level starts reducing, just top it back up again.

12. Once you have finished steaming your puddings, remove from the slow cooker and foil and if serving the same day; invert over a serving plate.

13. If serving the same day; bring the 150ml brandy to a simmer in a saucepan over a high heat. Transfer the brandy to a ladle, light and pour over the hot pudding. Once the flames have subsided, the pudding is ready to serve with cream and/or custard.

If you are making these puddings in advance, remove from the foil and wrap in clean foil before storing in a cool dark place.

If you wish to turn one or both of these puddings into a Christmas cake cover it with apricot jam, roll out the marzipan large enough to wrap around the pudding shape, smooth out any joins, cover the marzipan with further apricot jam, roll out the fondant icing and place over the top of the cake wrapping it neatly around and smoothing any edges or bulges. You can then place a couple of holly leaves on top for decoration.

Moreish Nibbles

Fudge

The most divine fudge recipe you'll ever try, I make this at Christmas time, I double the ingredients to make twice as much which then fills a Celebrations tin to the brim and is perfect to share with all the guests on Christmas Eve. I can guarantee the tin will be empty before Father Christmas arrives!

Ingredients

115g butter

150ml milk

397g can of condensed milk

450g demerara sugar

Using greaseproof paper; line a tin approx. 20cm square ready for the fudge mixture, I use a couple of loaf tins as they are the equivalent size.

Have a sugar thermometer to hand OR a shallow glass of cold water.

1. Using a large non-stick saucepan put all the ingredients into the pan starting with the butter and milks so that you don't burn the sugar and melt over a low heat, stirring with a wooden spoon until the sugar dissolves. Make sure your saucepan is much bigger as the mixture swells and boils like hot volcano lava.

2. Bring to the boil, it'll look like a witch's cauldron bubbling away so get ready to cast your spells.

3. At this point I put on an oven glove and for the next step as it gets really hot above the pan. Stirring continuously simmer for a further 10-15 minutes until it reaches 118°C on the sugar thermometer. If you don't have a thermometer fill a shallow glass with cold water a drop a little of the mixture into the water. If it's reached the right temperature it will form a soft ball of fudge in the bottom of the glass, if it is not ready then the mixture will disperse and cloudy the water so keep stirring and simmer the mixture for longer in the saucepan.

4. Once it reaches 118°C or forms a little fudge ball in the glass remove the fudge from the hob stir until it stops bubbling and then start beating with a wooden spoon. Keep beating it until it's very thick and starts setting on your spoon, it'll be a good 10-15 minutes beating before it starts setting. I usually take the pan outside into the garden and beat the mixture in the garden as it helps cool the mixture down quicker. It's a mixture of cooling and beating air into the fudge which makes it set.

4. Once it starts setting pour it into the lined greaseproof tin and leave it to cool. Allow it to cool at room temperature.

Once set cut into small squares and obviously pop at least one in your mouth to test - bakers' privileges.

Shortbread

Just what the doctor ordered after a cold winter's day on the boat, rosy red cheeks, cuppa in hand and a lovely slice of shortbread.

Ingredients

100g butter at room temperature

50g caster sugar plus extra to decorate

150g plain flour

Turn the oven on to 170°C while you make your mixture. Grease an 18cm loose bottomed round tin.

1. Cream the butter and sugar together.

2. Using a fork, gradually stir in the flour.

3. Using your fingertips, draw the mixture together.

4. Press the mixture into the greased tin.

5. Using the fork prongs, gently press around the edges of the tin to create a lined margin and gently prick all over to create a pattern.

6. Pop in the oven for approx. 20 minutes until it is the colour of pale straw.

7. Leave it to cool down in the tin for a few minutes before slicing into triangles and sprinkling with caster sugar.

8. Wait until it has completely cooled down before removing from the tin.

Oat Biscuits

My version of a hobnob, simple but effective and it almost feels healthy until you see how much sugar goes into the biscuits.

Ingredients

112g butter

128g demerara sugar

170g porridge oats

Turn the oven on to 180°C while you make your mixture. Grease a 20cm loose bottom round tin.

1. Using a non-stick saucepan; put the butter and sugar over a low heat and melt slowly until the sugar dissolves, stirring with a wooden spoon frequently to ensure the sugar doesn't burn on the bottom of the pan.

2. Take the saucepan off the heat and add the oats to the mixture. Stir well until it is evenly mixed.

3. Pour the oatie mix into the tin and press down firmly to compact the mixture.

4. Pop in the oven for 20 minutes.

5. Leave it to cool down for 10 minutes before cutting into triangle slices.

6. Store in an airtight container.

Gingerbread Men

Another one of Scotty's favourites. I personally cannot stand ginger but I do love making these just so I can decorate them and make each of them have their own individual characteristics.

Ingredients

100g plain flour

50g soft brown sugar

1tsp ground ginger

50g butter

1tbsp milk

2tbsp black treacle

Smarties or currents to decorate

½ cup of icing sugar

1-2tbsp water

Turn the oven on to 180°C while you make your mixture. Grease a baking tray.

1. Put the flour, sugar and ginger into a bowl and mix it all together evenly.

2. Put the butter, treacle and milk into a bowl and pop in the microwave on a medium to high setting for 45 seconds.

3. Take out the microwave and stir, if the butter has not completely melted, put it back in the microwave for 15 seconds and repeat until fully melted.

4. Make a well in the centre of the dry ingredients, pour the melted butter mixture into the well of the flour and mix together with a wooden spoon to form a soft ball.

5. Leave the mixture to cool until it is firm to touch.

6. Once it has cooled down, roll the mixture out onto a lightly floured surface to approx. 5mm thick.

7. Using a gingerbread man biscuit cutter cut out as many gingerbread men as the mixture will allow.

8. Using a spatula, transfer the gingerbread men to a greased baking tray evenly spaced apart to allow for them to spread during cooking and pop the tray in the oven for 15 minutes.

9. Remove from the oven and don't worry that they are still soft when you bring them out the oven, as they cool down they will get harder.

10. Wait 15 minutes before transferring them to a wire cooling rack.

11. While they are cooling down; mix the icing sugar with water to make a thick icing.

12. Using a knife, place a little bit of icing sugar to the back of the smarties and place on the gingerbread men for eyes, nose, mouth and button decorations. The icing is to act as glue to stick them down so it doesn't need to be seen.

13. Allow the icing to set the smarties in place and enjoy!

Absolute Necessities

Vanilla Butter Icing

This recipe makes enough to fill and sandwich a Victoria Sponge together or enough for 12 butterfly cake toppings.

Ingredients

300g icing sugar

100g butter

1tsp vanilla essence

1. Pour icing sugar into a bowl.

2. Add the butter on top.

3. Using the back of a fork; compress the butter into the icing and keep doing so until it starts to combines into butter and form a stiff paste

4. Add the vanilla essence.

Lemon Curd

This recipe comes in very handy to bribe my father in law with when I want help fixing my boat, it's his favourite!

Ingredients

100g butter

225g granulated sugar

3 eggs plus 1 egg yolk

9tbsp lemon juice

1. Melt the butter in a saucepan over a low heat.

2 Add the sugar, eggs, yolk and lemon juice and stir in.

3. Cook on a medium to low heat until the curd thickens. It should coat the back of a spoon; at this point remove from the heat straight away.

4. Pour the curd into clean, dry jars and cover. Eat within 2 weeks of making, but I'll guarantee it won't last 2 weeks in our house!

80

Chocolate Butter Icing

This recipe makes enough to fill and sandwich the chocolate cake together as well as ice the top too.

Ingredients

400g icing sugar

200g butter

100g cocoa powder

1. Pour the icing sugar into a bowl.

2. Add the butter on top.

3. Using the back of a fork; compress the butter into the icing and keep doing so until it starts to combines into the butter.

4. Add the cocoa powder and repeat until it is evenly mixed.

5. Use to fill and top your chocolate cake spreading evenly with a knife.

Chocolate Cream Fondant

This works great as a creamy filling for chocolate cake.

Ingredients

284ml double cream

300g dark chocolate

1. Whisk the cream in a bowl until it forms stiff peaks.

2. Break up the chocolate into small squares and place in a bowl.

3. Put the chocolate into the microwave onto a medium to high heat setting for 1 minute.

4. Take out the microwave and stir, if not completely melted, put back in the microwave for 30 seconds and repeat until fully melted.

5. Wait until the chocolate has cooled down slightly.

6. Turn the whisk onto a low speed and start whisking the cream whilst slowly adding melted chocolate to the cream. Keep whisking until it's fully blended and even in colour.

7. Use to fill and top your chocolate cake spreading evenly with a knife and be sure to store in the fridge.

8. Don't forget to lick the bowl out before washing up!

Marzipan

This recipe will make approx. 565g marzipan.

Ingredients

450g ground almonds

3 eggs

¼ tsp salt

4tsp vanilla extract

3-4 cups of icing sugar

1. Separate the egg whites from the yolk and cast aside the yolks. If you are planning to make egg custard tarts then save the yolks for these.

2. Add the salt to the egg whites and whisk until it forms a frothy mixture.

3. Add the vanilla to the egg whites and whisk briefly.

4. Now stir in the ground almonds.

5. Adding one cup at a time, 3 cups of the icing sugar to the mixture and using the kneading whisks on a slow speed; knead the sugar in.

6. Using the last remaining cup of icing sugar, add bit by bit until it forms a smooth, pliable dough and discard any remaining sugar.

7. Divide the dough into 4 and wrap each ball of dough in cling film and then foil to keep it airtight.

Sweet Pastry

This recipe makes enough pastry for 12 Egg Custard Tart bases or 1 Bakewell case.

Ingredients

225g plain flour

110g butter at room temperature

80g caster sugar

2-3tbsp water

1. Put all the pastry ingredients into a bowl and using your fingertips rub the butter into the flour and sugar.

2. Once the mixture starts to form fine bread crumbs, using your hands, start to compress the mixture together adding water as required to form a ball of dough. It is very important that your butter is at room temperature otherwise the mixture will not form the right consistency.

3. Roll out the pastry onto a lightly floured surface.

83

Recipes

Use the following pages to write down your own favourite sweet recipes:

Recipes

Recipes

Recipes

Index

Acknowledgements

Thank you to Frostie for all the helpful book names, not all of which were suitable for the cover of a family recipe book but they certainly provided entertainment along the way.

Thank you to Simon for the winning recipe book name and all the input for the very important decisions within the book, i.e. helping decide which are Delicious Dinner Desserts and which fall into the category of Luscious Lunchbox Surprises. If Simon had his way they would all be Absolute Necessities!

Finally a big thank you to Scott for putting on a brave face and taking one for the team trying some of the not so nice trial and error recipes I've made along the way!

First published in Great Britain in 2017 by Stacey Belbin

Copyright © 2017 Stacey Belbin
ISBN 978-1-5272-1557-3

The moral right of the author has been asserted.

Cover Illustrations: Kristina Khlebnikova
Photography: Stacey Belbin
Design: Book Printing UK
Production: CLOC Ltd